Limited edition 211/400

To Karen.

Jo Kjaer first visited Norfolk in 1948 when she was five, after living in other parts of eastern England she settled here in the 1990's. During a varied career as designer, restaurateur, nutritionist, tutor, educational advisor and aid worker, articles on the history of food and special diets were published in magazines including Harpers & Queen, The Tatler and The Nutrition Practitioner. In 2007, she gained a first in the Advanced Poetry Diploma at the University of East Anglia and won the first Café Writers Norfolk Poetry Commission: *As the Crow Flies* is her first collection. She teaches Creative Writing for the National Extension College and is working towards a second collection inspired by the landscape and history of Norfolk.

*To Sylvia — a few
lines about
Norfolk with
best wishes
Jo Kjaer
April 2009.*

As
The
Crow
Flies

Jo Kjaer

Edited by Helen Ivory

GATEHOUSE PRESS LTD

Gatehouse Press Limited
Cargate Lane, Saxlingham Thorpe
Norfolk NR15 1TU
www.gatehousepress.com

First Published in Great Britain by
Gatehouse Press Limited 2008

Printed by the MPG Books Group
in the UK

ISBN (10 Digit) 0 9554770 6 9
ISBN (13 Digit) 978 0 9554770 6 5

Cover design by Lee Seaman, based on a painting by Nicola Hart

Gatehouse Press Team:

Tom Corbett, Ian Buck, Lee Seaman
Piers Blaikie, Claire Griffiths, Al Hammond, Jude Sayer

Contents

Foreword

As the Crow Flies is the product of the first Café Writers
Norfolk Commission. The Commission is a new annual
poetry competition open to recent graduates from a
creative writing based course at Norwich School of Art
and Design and the UEA. Patrons of the Commission,
Kate and Dominic Christian are passionate about Norfolk
and wanted to support emerging literary talent, and build
a body of poetry which responds to the county in some
way. They will generously donate £3,500 annually, for
the lifetime of Commission, which provides prize money
for the winner and funds the making of pamphlets such
as this.

The judges of the 2007 Café Writers Norfolk Commission
were patron Kate Christian, Chris Gribble Director of
the New Writing Partnership, Caroline Gilfillan Chair of
Poetry-next-the-Sea, and myself. One of the things that
we liked about Jo Kjaer's proposal was that she wanted
to give each poem an OS reference, anchoring it to the
particular place that inspired it. We liked also that
her writing voice has a sense of belonging; a spiritual
connection with the landscape.

Helen Ivory
Norwich, March 2008

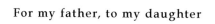For my father, to my daughter

Let any stranger find me so pleasant a county, such good ways ... I'll be once again a vagabond and visit them.

Sir Thomas Browne (17th century)

2

Aviatress *OS TF 898 304*

I dream of the speed of wings,
the ruffling of dark forces
around the heart: a beggar woman,
drawing shadow arcs on tree bark,
stealing feathers, polished in a mirror,
for her bed.

If I had this feather for a hand,
if this gamble lost me a stake
in ordinariness, only the hawk
would see the woman hidden
in my eye.

The Marsh Tit *OS TF 902 298*

I spend these pale days walking
the boardwalk to see the bird -
through avenues of rustling reed,
the sway creak of alder carr,
and flocks of little siskins
greening the air.

I wanted to tell you about this bird;
how he's dressed in a dust jacket -
his black cap reminds me of your beret,
jaunty, set over one eye,
when we packed for Paris;
his white collar, like a barristers tie,
tucked neatly under the neck,
lifts up in a wind.

And how the bird is shy and quick,
and quite ordinary, a dull utility
among robins and coral bramblings
in the copse. But, by my reckoning
he's a design classic – as cool as R Fiennes
or a pebble by Henry Moore;
a winter statement match furnishing
grey bark, buff grass and umber leaves.

I wanted you to know too
I like the view from the hide:
I like caps of moss on dead logs,
how pistol, style and stigma are buried
in the bud. and how *parus palustris*
keeps bringing me back to you
with his *did I – did I – did I ?*
so I can answer, *yes - you did.*

- Apologies to the Marsh Tit for turning his scolding song
di-di-di into *did I- did I- did I.*

The Prayer for Rain
*- In Judaism, Shemini Atzeret celebrates the planting
of crops in autumn.*

I grew up with seasonal planting:
each year at Shemini Atzeret,
black specks like dots of vanilla pod
were scattered in.
The prayer for rain was not said,
my family were Christian,
but my mother praised me
for watering the earth
as if I had talked to God.

My first patch was planted like a church -
the congregation chosen for piety and obedience;
lilies genuflected to the sun
and snowdrops dipped like nuns
praying under habits of snow.
Behind a willow screen,
where ivy climbed with rose,
I picnicked as a priest -
Hovis on a Morris 8 hubcap,
wine from a bottle of pop.

In the 70's I planted a mandala.
'nothing like the one we saw in Tibet'
he taunted.
Not a cheerful kaleidoscope,
a Persian carpet,
freckles of tortoiseshell,
a thousand tigers' eyes?
That night, during meditation,
a posse of lamas chased him
away over the Himalayas.

Now I have you; you're growing up
like this vast and wonderful garden –
an anarchy of colour -
all the shapes and forms
you try on aged four.

It's October and we've just scattered in
seeds, like dots of vanilla pod,
and I want you to know what I mean
when rain waters this plot of earth
and I hug you tight and sing.

Chlorophilia *OS TF 012 337*

In the time of new grass
I am in love:
that quick intake of breath,
the desire to ruffle his hair,
like plush velvet ,
upholstering the path
with more threads
than all the people in the world.

Nature

The twisting stem, the arcing flight,
the place left alone for a year,
like a deserted garden
goes back to itself without you.

Nothing remains of the nursery
we bought up that Sunday -
only the throttled stem
of the beloved bellflower
costing the earth.

Gaia *OS TG 185 433*

It was not our plan to pad the dog
or bark the fox,
or teach a hare to box.

No hands of ours sent chalk cliffs up,
or told how strange material
called ice should flow.

As if gardens of moss could be mine,
or the bones of mammoths,
asleep under your feet,
belong to you.

In a Glade

A hundred
pink foxgloves
freckled like a nose
stand still here.

A plip of rain
plays
one heavy sound
before bouncing
off one glove -
sets them going
like a carillon of bells.

A hundred
white foxgloves
freckled like a nose
stand still here.

A plip of rain
plays
one heavy sound
before bouncing
on one glove -
sets them off
like an audience
applauding.

Bluebell *OS TF 979 333*
After David Malouf

I'm making a new theorem:
this bluebell is blue
therefore there is no other colour,
you said.

As if nature's breath was blue,
passing over the wood,
transforming it
with a twitch of leaves.

Perhaps she carried the seeds
in her mouth and spat them out
recklessly, to push winter back,
you said.

This is a blue not of the night
or day, I said, it reminds me
of a small glass for eye drops
from Bristol, on the bathroom shelf.

I've got the hang of it now, you said,
I'm Persephone, lying down with spring.

Wildings *OS TF 965 354*
To John & Mary Parker

When you tip the jar
warm jelly
pulls to one side
under the skin
holds on like a graft
for a pip to escape
in the pale pink lake
as if flowers fell over the fruit.

All it had was old
a hand in the hedge
rain
air
the sky
and the field.

- 'wildings' – chance seedlings from pips of discarded domestic
apples

13

Baking Thoughts *OS TF 933 424*

Today, the dough has a new face
as if it needs to be pulled into
flat bread from Italy
or small steamed buns from Asia.

I wonder if the owl,
gliding through the old railway tunnel,
has any idea how closely its face
mimics the front of a steam engine.

Echo *OS TF 917 438*

In the car park,
the same sun wrinkled observers
video themselves, permanently waving,
and sons of men
with tiny children
still dangle bacon for the crab
that got away.

Spoon shaped dainty racers
and throaty old engines power home:
the tranquil lakes, those silver stars,
and blue sands that float
over treasure islands,
are all still there.

I look for me
in the place I left my childhood -
an echo of me still hums there.

Smoke Signal *OS TG 084 409*
For J H

We rode the predator through a jungle -
a rhinoceros not a fallen oak, miming;
friends who felt like brother and sister
playing on a sunlit stage.

You kept asking –
are you coming with me?

Straw faces, white bales round
like a foreign sausage,
conjured battles, war paint on plains.

We were very brave
through bracken,
goose stepping over adders.

When sun streams through the valley
peace is kept in the clouds
and blue sky, and in the mist,
which drifts here occasionally,
like the smoke signal
the day you went away.

Blood Line

Eventually,
we come to know
the matters of most of all;
the wind ceasing to breath
as the tide turns,
the same heart holding back
telling nothing brave,
nothing it hasn't told before.

Except, perhaps,
a rain drop from moss -
likely this is clear,
magnifying, slightly out of true,
the venous trail on the back
of a hand working in soil.

But it is me in the wood,
digging for a truffle -
my blood line back to you,
so I know where to go
and what to do.

Remember the Heat? *OS TF 675 424*

It's summer affecting us,
slowing down to empty
the brain - past thinking.

Clear sky and white sun burning
the right side of your face;
one cheek hot, one cheek cool.

Squinting at figures floating
through glare, on blond hills of sand,
red cliffs, spiky grass.

Can't remember anything
we said just 'the heat!'
flushing the air.

Shoreline *OS TF 858 458*

But, will you remember
the squeal of geese over us -
skeins threading clouds,
the dawn pale as an egg

as I waited for you
to undo the grass
and find me?

Camera *OS TF 219 425*

Someone else saw us
through the eye
of a square black box
as we smiled, and stiffened,

waiting for the click
that took our past,
catching it forever,
so that when we are very old

we will remember
to come back here,
and contemplate our lives,
on the blue canvas of the sea.

Home Ground

You go out about 6pm
and walk round your town,
every night a different direction.

East

Behind the allotments,
holly and ivy overhang the path -
armfuls of the red
against the green at Christmas,
ice crunching underfoot
like frozen tissue paper.

Now, in August, the lane's fruitful;
cherry plums and blackberries stain the path.
A squirrel dances about his stashes of food,
- a furry question mark
furnishing his winter sleep.

West

At the station crossroad,
a party assembles on the cable
strung over the field.
They come in singly,
to dot the line like fat commas,
pinions fanned
for the entry of a beak.

Done up like shiny boots,

flitting about, visiting,
one hops the queue,
sets them all off
leaping crow, jack, rook,
signals the take off en block.

North

Up the road the butchers click knives
to christen a body part. A leg or loin,
ribs or best end sit on the slab,
rolled and tied like red and white striped linen.

Zenith

They told us last night on TV
that SETI is detecting intelligent life on Mars,
and we're sending life forms
from the cliffs in Devon into space.

There may be other planets seeking life,
in the other one hundred billion galaxies,
who will find this broadcast,
leaking in their space,
a puzzling example.

Noesis

Sometimes, I'm afraid of the words
I come down to next morning -
there is the temptation
to stay inside a poem
and live in the imagined world -
a becoming, not a being.

Moor *OS TF 901 303*

                    Leaf free,
the colour of this place in winter
has every shade of light;
don't touch it with more than a wash
over the water.

Swimming *OS TG 048 453*

Rips of tide rock you shelf to shelf,
the breath of monsters bubble skin and hair,
use shingle for a comb, swish in the inner ear -
shaken by water to be itself.

Pulled up by the rusty tractor on the beach,
you stride out, your shadow huge,
some animal risen from the deep, flat textured,
long limbed, dark and wolf-hungry -
the world in front, that other element out of sight.

You left no trace when you swam its sea last night.

.

The Beach *OS TF 898 460*

Over the border,
away from neat villages
and green lanes,
the beach hisses and spits.

You're bowled along,
a thing of flailing limbs and wild hair,
a hostage to movement,
and anchorless in the ripping wind.

Posting the Rain *OS TG 085 435*

Words on clouds, dark weather
fogging the line lying under the sky;
a ruin on the cliff's edge blurring,
missing the spray of black wings rising
from the grazed meadow, the broken barley heads,
and the supermarket van aquaplaning round the bend,
will be read upside down by rain
- yourhomedelivery.com.
Words on rain rush into aquifers and creeks,
like fish fry swim over reed and gravel beds,
and in the message I would have sent you,
drop, letter by letter, into the North Sea,
posting themselves to Denmark,
The Hague, and every foreign port in between.

November *OS TG 045 440*

Nearly winter - its first breath curling
around butter lying cold on the plate,
on the acreage of trees, where we walk,
their tight permed tops of leaves
browning the earth;
chills an uncamouflaged bee
bumping on a window in the sleepy village.

It's nearly here –
rabbits tremble in pockets of moss,
the crooked pines and towers of churches,
tall as alexanders in spring, stand,
and over the rise, the masts of schooners,
landlocked by tide, meet grey afternoons
we spend in tea shops empty of tourists
before the light leaves the sky.

Arms *OS TG 181 071*
For Robert Creeley

I feel some empathy with the ficus
drooping in a corner of this small sanitised city
where sons are born and old women die.

But I don't want to acclimatise
to the hum of machinery,
and figures carrying urine bags.

I want to remember youth and power,
and the smile from a handsome ambulance driver
now everyone keeps taking my arm.

But I fall asleep on the X ray table,
struggle to open the sandwich wrapper at lunch
and hold the plastic cup upright to drink.

I forget so easily how we have
to do the unimaginable.

taking your arm, their arms, taking them in your arms,

South Creake Church *OS TF 866 363*

We sat beneath angels
and listened to a quartet:
Beethoven uncoiled in the air -
four bows tuning the mind,
one voice playing over and over,
until we were deaf.

Little Wood *OS TF 979 333*

Out of the sun,
this morning,
away from the blink
of standby machinery,
I ducked under
skyscraper trees
to break open
the pool of algae,
with a stone.

Good Friday April 07 *OS TF 979 333*

On this cold spring day,
a dry verse about abandonment;
the break in a palm
or the delicate bone of the foot
which we hear, or think we hear
as a stem snaps in the wood.

Crow *OS TF 984 216*

Mouse, snail and chafer tremble;
fingers of wings, half sky,
half bird - a vibration,
sun risen to her *krra, krra, krra,*
raking death from mould.

Drills down fast like a bradawl,
crowbar feet, beak heavy with marrow.
Quills flutter, new crimson dew drops,
little by little, life behind the rooky wood.

In the space between leaves
satellites hum to sleep black fruit:
even they have ceased to breath.

As the Crow Flies *OS TG 043 333*

Follow the outlaw! Do I know her for a crow?
Her name is nothing; a black utility drilling sextons
geometric suit, a flapping windbag cawing
at chimney pots and hornpies crests.

Do I see the devils' murder in the fenny copse,
the fisher of dung, or her wrinkle round my eye,
her body on a crowstick,
or a journeywoman outwitting the gun?

Dig deeper for wings blackening the wind,
the dark brown iris of a corbeau
jinked here from Asia under a flat harder sun.
A roving ticket holder from steppe to farmland,

code breaker of countries, brain teasing whelks,
the semaphore of washing lines,
another Denmark gyring over mammoths -
an ordinary bird?

Vanishing Point *OS TF 890 450*

We promenade past the sentry box
and Lady Ann's poplars,
alongside dogs and dancing children,
through five barred gates,
to the boardwalk, litter bins,
pines and moss garden.

Those that know it quieten down,
send up the unfinisheable poem
to the blue ceiling, rewrap scarves,
taste the first familiar muddy tang
before pulling up the ridge
above the meals.

Silenced by space!
Alone with the memory of water -
so far out figures on the horizon
appear like dots walking pin dogs
towards the sea.

Imagine a young Giotto painting us
before perspective - twenty three walkers
with barking dogs looking at a party
of naturists displayed on pillows of sand.
No one could vanish
over the horizon or into the dunes.

Homecoming *OS TF 946 409*

A painting of the hill fort
hangs over our bed.
I follow each brush stroke,
pulled in at night by the collar of stone
to learn the nook and snick of the axe,
the flint chipped height of the wall
you built to keep me in.

But I am not contained:
I blink for the enclosure to open,
like an eye facing the sea,
dilating its pupil to read the flats
              and open water,
and the soft flicking
feathers of a thousand birds.

And it must be these,
just before dawn,
              calling me,
as they lift and whirl -
pale flakes of ash weave the sky -
              waiting to leave,
scattering seeds in the ditch -
              wild flower, barley, rye.

Some days, I'm left in the fort -
                    the map is useless,
a brain before bronze can't read.
                    Today,
 I'm half here, half there -
slapping dough on a stone,
watering fire to steam clams -
sweet flesh for a crisp new wine,
          and your homecoming –
wanting you,
                    differently,
hardy, dark, lean as a bough,
                    unbound.

Allowance

Sometimes, we long for the panic
when each went away.
Until remembering
the last dish we shared:
a party on a crumb
twin salad leaves,
being neither full nor empty,
we licked lips that will never kiss again
drifting further and further apart
like two feathers on the tide,
one going out, one coming in.

6/09/07 In Church *OS TF 866 363*

If this is where time and this world meet eternity,
they met here at three o'clock
on a September afternoon,
with music thrusting toward a place
that may have, a few hours ago,
steadied Pavarotti to cross the threshold.

Bixes Lane *OS TG 071 411*

Tonight, in the west,
the sun went down
on the right side of Bixes Lane:
I wonder how long before my soul
takes me there,
to the edge of colour:
I wonder if it has a name,
like this lane,
and whether my soul will come in
or leave me there.

This Life

            has been lived
before I was assembled
inside the sleeves of love.
It has nothing to do with
candlewick, or christening,
nothing to do with tribe -
more like a yearning for wildness;
the tattoo in the wolves throat
homing the pack, or the engine of lionness
that beats the strides of zebra
through tall grass.

This walk has been walked
before I found it,
hailed it a discovery and came back.
It has nothing to do with season,
or exercise, or looking,
nothing to do with being seen
but more like swinging a hand
over a bed of nettles,
so fast the pendulum spills pollen
on graves of acorn and glass.

This death has been done
before I say goodbye.
It has nothing to do with reapers,
or grimness, or age,
nothing to do with graves -
maybe it's like
the lights on a runway
blinking,
or suddenly being free from memory
as in a fugue.
Maybe, a door opens.

And so we leave nothing behind:
we've been here as a feather
lifting in a breeze
over the land.

Acknowledgements

My father gave me Norfolk when I was five – it is home, and inspiration for this book.

I owe the Café Writers Norfolk Commission a huge thank-you for the financial support to walk the footpaths of the Glaven and Wensum Valley in preparation for this collection. In particular, the patrons, Kate and Dominic Christian, Helen Ivory, whose editing pencil was perceptive and always good humoured, Tom Corbett, who navigated a smooth path through the machinery of publication via Gatehouse Press as well as adopting my overgrown fig tree, Martin Figura for photography, Nicola Hart, whose painting of Figsbury Hill became the inspiration for the cover of *As The Crow Flies* and Lee Seaman for the final cover design.

Significant others whose encouragement was invaluable include Sarah Law and my fellow students at UEA. I am also indebted to Nigel Larkin for explaining the geology of Norfolk.

Chlorophilia first appeared as *In the time of* in *Gift;*
The Prayer for Rain appeared in *Not Expecting Fish,* both anthologies published by Gatehouse Press.

OS references in these poems refer to their locations on Ordnance Survey maps. For more information, visit www.ordnancesurvey.co.uk.

Also from Gatehouse Press

Lunatic Moon – Jenny Morris

"Jenny Morris' poems stand at the edges of forests following the trails of fairy-tales, noting occasions of unhappiness. Stepmothers and stepchildren, husbands and wives dealing with furies, powers of transformation, spells, losses. It is not a comfortable world, nevertheless it presents itself and has to be faced calmly, wittily. The dangerous enchanted forest opens on to American scenes, wider, less closed in by history and myth, then leads to a few expressly lighter poems, but the overall tone is rich and dark: it is the sane end of the lunatic moon."

George Szirtes

Another Kissing Couple Has Exploded

– Gary Kissick

Gary Kissick wittily leads the reader on a quest of exploration; from the tormented bliss of resurrected memories and emotional reflection, through gleeful cultural clashes and cherished events in foreign climbs, to the idiosyncrasies of dislocation in Norfolk via slabs of Americana, both archetypal and modern. He draws on rich experiences to create a deeply personal collection of poems steeped in deadly dry humour and evocative emotional connection.

Not Expecting Fish – edited by Charles Christian

An anthology of poetry by students of the University of East Anglia Creative Writing Diploma Course 2007.

"The poems in this book deal with the viscera of life. From Joanna Clark's Pink, Yellow, Red disturbing domestic mother and daughter scene, to Judy Lawther's very moving Waiting Rooms, on the death of her father, to pick out just two. This is what poetry is for – to explore what we are; what makes us tick – to capture the unsayable and make it sing."

Helen Ivory

Gift – edited by Tom Corbett and Helen Ivory

A sensuous scarlet, suede-feel hardback embossed with just the title "gift" in gold, *Gift* is a beautifully produced book of original love poems by local writers ranging from the internationally renowned, such as George Szirtes, right through to previously unpublished poets. It is a wide-ranging look at love in all its many aspects and the fifty plus poems included are by turns, thoughtful, touching, moving and funny.

Buy these books direct from our website:

www.gatehousepress.com